JAMES DEAN

JAMES DEAN

Timothy Jacobs

JG PRESS

Published in the USA 1994 by JG Press
Distributed by World Publications, Inc.

The JG Press imprint is a trademark of
JG Press, Inc.
455 Somerset Avenue
North Dighton, MA 02764

Produced by
Brompton Books Corporation
15 Sherwood Place
Greenwich, Connecticut 06830

ISBN 1-57215-033-5

Printed in Slovenia

Designed by Tom Debolski
Edited and captioned by
Timothy Jacobs

Page 1: A highly melodramatic Warner Brothers
publicity still for the epic motion picture, *Giant*.
Here, James Dean and Elizabeth Taylor are in
character for their roles as Jett Rink and Leslie
Benedict.
Pages 2-3: James Dean, in character as his
unforgettable persona Jim Stark. This publicity still
for the Warner Brothers film, *Rebel Without a
Cause*, captures the intense, introspective quality
that so well suited James Dean for the role.

CONTENTS

INTRODUCTION

If I could have just one day when I wasn't all confused . . . If I felt I belonged some place . . . . – James Dean as Jim Stark in **Rebel Without a Cause**

Above: **The teenage 'Jimmy' Dean with fellow members of the Fairmount, Indiana, American Legion youth baseball team.**
At right: **A theatrical agency photograph of James Dean, circa 1951-52, in his early New York days. Even in this stock photo, Jimmy's deep-set eyes betray an unusual combination of knowledge, naivete and wariness.**

The life of James Dean has been the stuff of myth for four decades now. It could be said that 'The Life of James Dean' was a script that existed in the actor's *own* mind from childhood on. Indeed, grandma Emma Dean commented on his boyhood: 'Even then, Jimmy seemed to be able to be another person!'

James Byron Dean was born in Marion, Indiana, on 8 February 1931, the son of Winton and Mildred Dean. In 1935, Winton – a dental technician – was transferred to Sawtelle Veteran's Hospital in Santa Monica, California. In this new home, Jimmy's favourite pastime was playing with figures on a miniature theater stage, improvising plays with his mother. She died of cancer, when he was nine, in 1940.

His wife's illness had exhausted Winton's financial resources, and he had to send Jimmy back to Indiana, to live on a farm with his aunt and uncle, Ortense and Marcus Winslow, near the village of Fairmount.

Jimmy's first dramatic debut was a recitation for the Fairmount Women's Christian Temperance Union. He went on to other recitations and dramatic roles, including that of 'Grandpa Vanderholf' in a high school production of *You Can't Take It With You*. Under the tutelage of high school drama coach Adeline Nall, he won the Indiana State Dramatic Contest with a monologue entitled 'The Madman.'

Graduating from Fairmount High in 1949, he went to stay with his father in Southern California, and enrolled in Santa Monica City College, switching to the University of California – Los Angeles (UCLA) Drama Department in 1950. He then got an apartment with his acting friend Bill Bast. They double-dated Jeannette Lewis and Beverly Wills: Jimmy and Beverly's relationship lasted until his departure for New York.

He played Malcolm in a UCLA production of *Macbeth*, and his first professional acting job was a commercial for Coca-Cola, with co-stars Nick Adams and Beverly Long Dorff. Other early television appearances included the role of St John, on 'Father Ryan's Television Theater,' with co-stars Gene Lockhart, Michael Ansara, Ruth Hussey and Roddy McDowell. Jimmy also worked in radio, and had bit parts in several movies: *Fixed Bayonets, Sailors Beware* (with Dean Martin and Jerry Lewis) and **Has Anybody Seen My Gal?** (with Rock Hudson and Charles Coburn).

James Whitmore gave a series of lessons on the Stanislavsky Method in the winter and spring of 1950-51, and Jimmy attended. At Whitmore's suggestion, he left for New York's intensive acting scene in the fall of 1951. At one point he worked as a stunt tester (along with the young Warren Oates) for 'Beat the Clock.'

He soon became involved with dancer Dizzy Sheridan, and not long after meeting her, he and actress Christine White co-auditioned for Lee Strasberg's prestigious Actors Studio (spelled without an apostrophe for a touch of *panache*). Jimmy and Christine were the only two chosen of 150 aspirants. He was still preparing for the life-role of *James Dean*.

Talent agent Jane Deacy had him working steadily in television: during his brief but spectacular career, he had at least 14 major roles in television vehicles with such co-stars as Natalie Wood, Eddie Albert and Ronald Reagan.

Jimmy's first Broadway role was as the 'nature boy' Wally Wilkins in *See the Jaguar*, with Arthur Kennedy. The show opened on 3 December 1952, and 'James Dean' got rave reviews for his acting. His second venture on the 'Great White Way' won him a prestigious Antoinette Perry, or 'Tony,' Award for his portrayal of the corrupt servant Bachir in Andre Gide's *The Immoralist*, which opened on 1 February 1954.

He had by then auditioned for his first major motion picture role, in an adaptation of John Steinbeck's **East of Eden**. As friends Martin Landau and Billy Gunn and new paramour Barbara Glenn wished him luck, he struck out again for Southern California – where his legend was to take root and grow.

The triumph and the failure. *Above:* James Dean and Geraldine Page in their roles as Bachir and Marcelline from the Broadway production of Andre Gide's *The Immoralist. At right:* Jimmy as Malcolm in the UCLA production of *Macbeth*.

These pages: The young actor. Jimmy was always doing 'bits' – creating a dramatic moment whenever the chance arose. Whether walking in the street or spending time in one of his typically one-room residences, James Dean was almost always theatrically expressive.

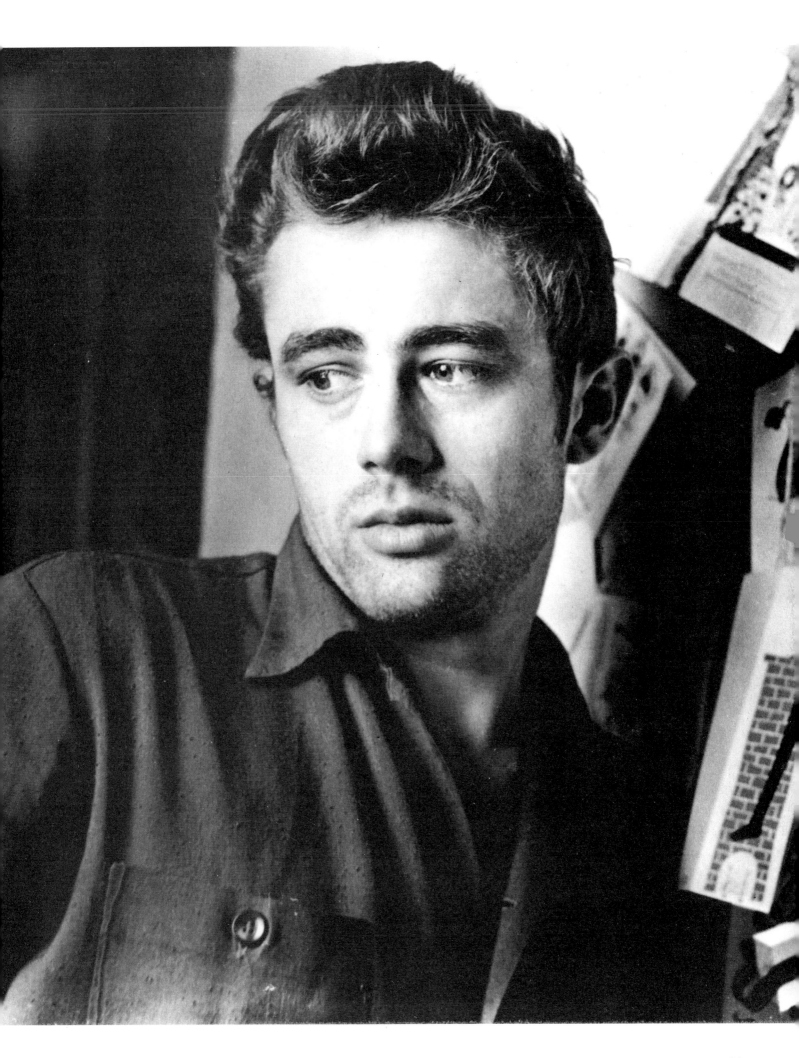

EAST OF EDEN

– Where is Aron?
– I don't know – I'm not my brother's keeper.
– Adam Trask (Raymond Massey) and Caleb Trask (James Dean)

Above: James Dean as Caleb Trask in *East of Eden*. In this scene, he is watching his estranged mother, Kathy Trask (Jo Van Fleet), put her earnings as a madam in the bank.
At right: A publicity still for *East of Eden*. Here – in character as Caleb Trask and his brother's unfaithful fiancee, the coquettish Abra – are James Dean and Julie Harris.

James Dean's portrayal of Caleb Trask in *East of Eden* was his first role in a major motion picture. Caleb or 'Cal' Trask is a misunderstood, misunderstanding person like, but with far more depth than, Sartre's narrator in *Nausea*. Elia Kazan's screen adaptation dealt with the last one-sixth of Steinbeck's book – in which Caleb and his brother Aron (played by Dick Davalos), the sons of Adam Trask (Raymond Massey), have a confrontation similar to the Biblical story of Cain and Abel, with several major twists.

The novel makes clear that the boys' mother, Kathy Trask (played by Jo Van Fleet), was unfaithful to their father with his own brother, Charles, and hints that one of the boys is the offspring of Adam, and the other, of Charles. In the film, we pick up when the boys' mother, having left the family when they were born, is a dim – but soon to be awakened – memory.

One day, Cal meets his mother, who now runs a brothel, in Monterey, and a telling dialogue ensues. Cal tells her that his brother Aron 'looks like you.' She then replies, 'Well, is he like me?' Cal answers 'No, he's good . . . I'm more like you.'

Cal comes to feel that his father never forgave himself for loving Kathy, and consequently is incapable of loving Cal – essentially putting him in the same category as her. Cal alternately rebels against, and seeks, his father's love. He is a confused, sensually-oriented youth, and it seems he can do nothing right – while his brother can do nothing wrong, in their father's eyes.

Caleb/Cain symbolically 'slays' Aron/Abel by taking him to his mother's whorehouse, and introducing him to her. However, Caleb repents his action, and opens his heart to his father's grief – his first action performed out of understanding for more than himself – and thus becomes worthy of his father's love. It will still be a rough road, but 'the way has been cleared.'

In the closing scene, the family is seeking someone to take care of their father, now an invalid. The father says to Cal, 'Don't get anybody else. You stay with me. You take care of me.'

'Jimmy,' as James Dean was affectionately known, chose a seemingly awkward time to state his intention to take up the role of Cal Trask. He made the announcement on the highly successful first night of *The Immoralist*, a fact that caused director Daniel Mann to bear a long resentment. Despite Jimmy's concomitantly short playing time in *The Immoralist*, Jimmy was to win a Tony Award for his portrayal of Bachir.

At the time, no one could understand his leaving a successful production. Jimmy's move proved to be a wise one, as his portrayal of Caleb Trask would establish him as a major big screen actor, and led to his nomination for an Academy Award, or 'Oscar.' (In fact, Jimmy's co-star Jo Van Fleet won the Best Supporting Actress Academy Award for the film).

Director Kazan remembered James Dean from his days with the Actors Studio. He had struck Kazan as a loner – stubborn, sulky and proud. These very qualities recommended Jimmy for the role of Caleb Trask. Kazan himself was fresh from a triumph with the Academy Award-winning motion picture **On the Waterfront**, which established the movie reputation of another Method actor – Marlon Brando, who won the Best Actor Academy Award for his role in that film.

Jimmy screen-tested for **East of Eden** with up-and-coming actor Paul Newman. Jimmy won the role, and Newman went on to star in such prestigious films as **The Long Hot Summer** and **Cat on a Hot Tin Roof**.

Kazan's attitude toward his own father colored the production and direction of **East of Eden**. Steinbeck hadn't intended the rise of an anti-hero in his novel, but Kazan wanted to focus on and underscore the tensions between father and sons. This distinct reduction of the sprawling epic later led

Below: **A still of the long-frustrated Caleb on the edge of frenzy and 'astride the horses of passion.' The publicity still** *at right* **literally captures Jimmy/ Caleb in the depths of the psychological whirlpool in which he has become trapped.**

a reviewer for *Time* magazine to comment on the finished film: 'They've taken the novel and stuffed it into a tight little psychoanalytical pigeon hole – a father problem.' As a counterbalance to that estimation, John Steinbeck, upon seeing the film, commented 'I think it'll be a classic.'

Kazan felt, when casting was complete, that Jimmy would naturally conflict with the staid, conservative Raymond Massey, who, in the role of Adam, was at odds with Jimmy's Caleb. Indeed, Massey did object to Jimmy's 'surliness' on the set (actually an inwardness born of his Method training, which asked an actor to 'sink into himself').

This proximity of director and actor was further intensified by the fact that *East of Eden* was shot on a closed set, so that Jimmy was essentially cloistered in the early stages of production. Then, in order to further 'methodize' their roles, Jimmy and Dick Davalos hung out together – in character – which helped to increase the 'fraternal' tension between them.

One thing he did not have to dig far for was the feeling of being cast off that Caleb Trask feels, given Jimmy's own family history. A crucial moment in the film is set up by Adam's scheme to send their Salinas Valley lettuce to the East Coast, which was then a novel approach to solving the seasonal greens shortage felt by Easterners. The plan fails, and Adam loses all his money.

Below: A between-scenes still on the set of *East of Eden*. With shaving cream and razor in his hand, perhaps Jimmy had a late night before that day's filming.

At right: Cal asks his father's approval of his idea to use a chute to unload the lettuce from the train. In typically unthinking and self-destructive style, Cal has stolen the chute from the train's coal tender.

Prompted by the rumors of a blazing new star, Metro-Goldwyn-Mayer Studios (MGM) starlet Pier Angeli visited the Warner lot after a 'shoot' on the *East of Eden* set one day, hoping to get a glimpse of Jimmy. It was love at first sight. They became very serious about each other, but since she was from a conservative Italian family, they had to keep their romance low-key, and spent their time together in hideaways along the Pacific Coast.

Shooting on *East of Eden* was wrapped up in August 1954, and Jimmy went for a quick trip to New York. Just as he returned, Pier announced her engagement to singer Vic Damone. Whether it was parental pressure, or Jimmy's sometimes unpredictable behavior that caused this sudden departure is not known: their love had seemed idyllic until that 'fatal moment.' What is clear, however, is what Pier expressed about Jimmy nearly 15 years later, after two divorces:

'He is the only man I ever loved deeply as a woman should love a man.'

Jimmy was broken up by this bizarre turn of events, and later said: 'I figure that when I went back to New York after finishing *East of Eden* her family and friends got her ear and changed her mind about me. . . . '

Perhaps James Dean was victimized in his ill-fated love affair by the very

James Dean carried around a lot of intensity when at work on a character. The studio still *at left* conveys some sense of this. He was always concentrating on the various aspects of the character – why he did what he did, when he did it, and how.

So much of it was related to his own experience that perhaps, at times, the dividing line between acting and reality blurred. This was quite clear in the utter naturalness with which he acted out such scenes as that *above*.

thing, that device, that he had used for self-protection, and as a tool of art, for most of his life. James Dean was indeed now the 'outsider' and had in fact become locked out of the very family – he and Pier – that he had so craved, just as Caleb Trask had been!

Then, compounding the irony was a role he played in the 'off time' after the completion of **East of Eden**. In a television production, **I Am a Fool**, with co-star Natalie Wood, he played a man who makes up his own identity to impress a high-class social circle he's just stumbled into.

He, as Walter Matthers, falls in love with a girl named Lucy; but shortly after, she has to go home. She boards the train before they've exchanged addresses, and before he can tell her his true name. She blurts out ecstatically as the train leaves the station that she will write him – but of course her letter will never reach him, addressed to the fictional name she knows him by.

The only girl Jimmy dated consistently after his star-crossed affair with Pier was Ursula Andress, freshly arrived from Europe, and, one suspects, in her European mannerisms, probably reminiscent of Pier.

East of Eden was released in the spring of 1955, to mixed reviews. Its first opening in New York was as a benefit for the Actors Studio, and guests paid $150 per ticket, with Marlene Dietrich, Anita Loos, Eva Marie Saint and Terry Moore as 'celebrity usherettes.'

Guest of honor James Dean was not there, however, as he and pals Martin Landau and Bill Gunn had seen the movie earlier, at the Astor Theater in

At left: James Dean in a General Electric Television Theater drama.
Above: A gauzy still of Ursula Andress, who was Jimmy's 'steady' after Pier Angeli. The contrast between the two is marked (see page 25), yet it's possible that European Ursula reminded Jimmy of European Pier.
Above left: James Dean in character as Jeff Latham, an innocent hitchhiker who is duped into working for a pair of ruthless hoodlums, in the 1955 television drama *The Unlighted Road*.

Times Square. He then became so nervous about the premier at the Actors Studio that he fled to Fairmount, Indiana, to see his adoptive parents, Marcus and Ortense Winslow, before heading back to Hollywood.

He now had a contract with Warner Brothers for nine films over a six-year period. The reviews of **East of Eden** went all the way from the *Library Journal's* 'One of the best films of this or any year . . .' to *The New York Times*' '. . . The solution is arbitrary. . . .' Still others pilloried Elia Kazan for perceived directorial excesses.

The one personage they could absolutely not ignore was James Dean as Cal Trask. While one reviewer panned him as 'a mass of histrionic gingerbread,' still others were enthralled with what they perceived as a clearly emergent talent. Hollywood columnist Hedda Hopper wrote: '. . . I sat spellbound. I couldn't remember ever having seen a young man with such power . . . so much sheer invention as this actor.'

James Dean had already signed a contract with Warner Brothers to do the panoramic saga **Giant**. Immediately, though, James Dean would have a chance to further deepen the public perception of his acting ability with his next film project: the classic **Rebel Without a Cause**.

Below: James Dean, Dick Davalos and Julie Harris, in character.
At right: Adam Trask to Caleb Trask: 'I'd be happy if you'd give me something like your brother's given me – something honest . . . and good.' Eventually, Cal does.

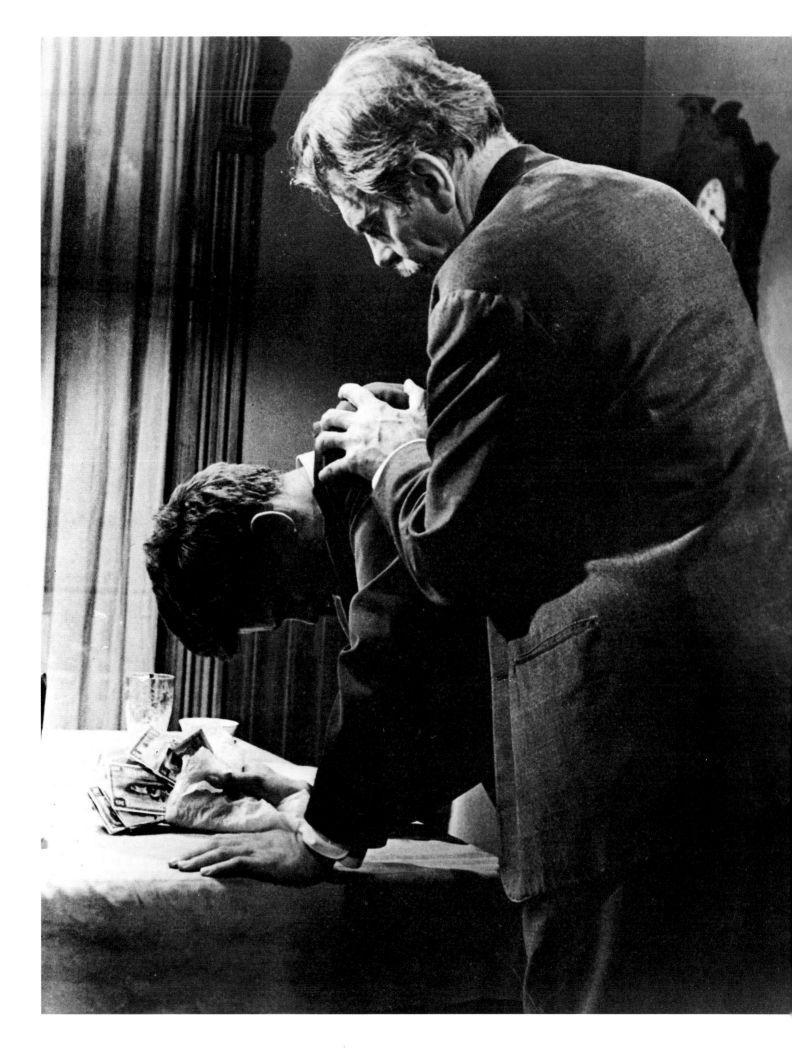

REBEL WITHOUT A CAUSE

– What can you do when you have to be a man? . . . You are going to stop me dad?
– You know I never stop you from anything.
– Jim Stark (James Dean) and his father (Jim Backus)

Rebel Without a Cause went into production in March, 1955. *Above:* A publicity still of James Dean as Jim Stark.
At right: An archetypal image of James Dean as Jim Stark. His every gesture conveyed a sense of the character, even in this publicity still: yet here is also seen an essential facet of Jimmy's own self.

Rebel Without a Cause is a film that portrays the classic problem of the questing youth, like a knight of old trying – against all odds – to find his way to the 'grail' of his rightful place in the 'kingdom' of adulthood. It also examines what happens when authority breaks down, and chaos rules.

Indeed, Jimmy's acting resonated mightily in materialistic, postwar America, where many parents abdicated their roles, and where many kids were taught values as children that they were later told to ignore. Teenagers across the land identified heavily with James Dean's character, Jim Stark.

Jim Stark, the new boy at Dawson High, faces a set of hurdles that are classic in their array: the girl next door snubs him; a tough and violent 'in crowd' menaces him; and he gets in trouble with the police.

Add to that Jim Stark's having to leave his previous school because he 'messed some kid up,' plus a less-than-effective father and a domineering mother, and you have the basic ingredients for a classic story of disaffected adolescence.

Rebel Without a Cause was inspired by Dr Robert M Lindner's book detailing the disintegration of a teenage psychopath, who, overwhelmed by violent memories of his own childhood, commits murder. Warner Brothers bought the movie rights to the book in 1946, and originally cast Marlon Brando in the lead role. Because of scripting problems, that production of 'Rebel' was terminated, and the property languished until 1954.

Juvenile delinquency was big news on the front pages of early 1950s newspapers, and Hollywood decided to bank on this post-war phenomenon, with low-budget blockbusters like *Blackboard Jungle* and *The Wild One*.

Nicholas Ray had just directed a box office hit called *Johnny Guitar*. Ray had an idea that not only could Warner Brothers 'cash in' on juvenile delinquency, they might be able to do some good by getting at the roots of it. Warner Brothers agreed, and Nicholas Ray was given the go-ahead for a completely new production.

Far from being a film in which 'all the blame is laid on the parents,' Ray did a masterful job of evincing the twin notions of moral responsibility and forgiveness that lead to the healing of James Stark's bruised psyche.

Ray wanted to cast his movie with kids – not accomplished actors necessarily, but young people who knew what the juvenile delinquent

scene was all about. James Dean, with his sensitivity and complex inner tension, was a natural for the vulnerable, yet explosive, Jim Stark.

Judy, Jim's romantic interest, was played by Natalie Wood; Jim Stark's dad was played by Jim Backus; his mom was played by Ann Durand; Plato – a kid who was even more of an emotional mess than Jim Stark – was played by Sal Mineo. The members of the 'in crowd' were portrayed as follows: Corey Allen was Buzz, the leader of the gang; Beverly Long was Helen; Nick Adams was Cookie; Dennis Hopper was Goon; Frank Mazzola was Crunch; Jack Simmons was Moose; Steffi Skolsky was Mil; Tom Bernard was Harry; and Jack Grinnage was Chick.

An 'actors' director,' Ray gave Jimmy a lot of leeway in the course of shooting the film. Jim Backus later said 'May I say that this is the first time in the history of motion pictures that a 24-year-old boy, with only one movie to his credit, was practically the co-director. Jimmy insisted on utter realism, and looking back, I sometimes wonder how we finished so violent a picture without someone getting seriously injured.'

Ray and scriptwriter Leon Uris (who later left the production, his script re-written by Irving Schulman) spent long hours interviewing delinquents in the lockup of the Culver City Police Department.

They then interviewed the kids' parents; and then the arresting officers. Out of this pool of information, a script was formed. Ray had the idea that the film would be an ensemble effort, with everyone contributing freely, and with the director providing a 'map' of dialogue and story line, while the acting would be spontaneous, as he felt befitted such a film as **Rebel Without a Cause**.

Meanwhile, Jimmy, having completed **East of Eden**, had to move from

Below: Jim Stark and gangleader Buzz (Corey Allen), between takes of the film's penultimate 'Chickie Run,' in which he and Buzz race stolen cars toward an ocean cliff: the last one to jump from his car wins – or suffers the ultimate loss (as did poor Buzz).
At right: Natalie Wood, James Dean and Frank Mazzola in a candid still. Natalie played Judy, who was Jim Stark's love interest, and Frank played a gangmember named 'Crunch.'

the Warner Brothers lot. He had a penchant for simple, one or two room abodes, and located a large A-frame house in Los Angeles suburb of Sherman Oaks. The place was basically a giant room with a balcony and a sleeping alcove.

While Jimmy made a big show of 'not giving a damn,' and gave every evidence of being an exceptionally abrasive character, it was all just a 'bit,' or mental game, that he played to get a rise out of people – as with the 'telephone trick' in Dick Clayton's office. It was also an unorthodox way of testing his own acting ability: 'Were people convinced by my actions?'

It could also vastly complicate his relations with other people. His was an already over-complicated personality, as Jimmy was 'on stage' every moment, except when deeply affected by someone, or when with the very closest of friends. At such moments, he could 'drop the act' and be astonishingly simple and open.

One evening, a recently-made friend, Joe Hyams, offered to introduce Jimmy to Humphrey Bogart. Jimmy readily accepted, and spent the evening sitting at Bogart's feet in awe, while the older actor held forth on a variety of subjects. James Dean, star-struck as any tourist, had more of a capacity for respect and reverence than he is generally given credit for.

Of his early teacher in 'The Method,' James Whitmore, he said: 'I owe a lot to Whitmore. . . . He told me I didn't know the difference between acting as a soft job and acting as a difficult art. . . . He made me see myself. He opened me up, gave me the key.'

As for the supporting cast in 'Rebel,' Jim Backus was fresh from supply-

At left: James Dean, in a very artistic pose, which, with its combination of brooding melancholy and unorthodox hand position, is an evocative variation on Auguste Rodin's famous sculpture 'The Thinker.' Just as 'The Thinker' was a man in suspension, and thus ever distant from home in any environment, so, too was James Dean – a man suspended in his brilliant portrayals of cinematic characters who were powerfully affecting, but yet not quite real.
Above: Director Nicholas Ray, Natalie Wood, James Dean and Ann Durand. Ray was an 'actor's director,' and believed in naturalistic expression. This, coupled with his desire for cinematic realism, meshed with Jimmy's vision of film production perfectly.

Above: Natalie Wood, as Judy, and James Dean, as Jim Stark, in a publicity still from *Rebel Without a Cause.*

At far right: Sal Mineo and Jimmy in character on the set of same. This film brought together an astonishing array of young acting talent – please see the text.

ing the voice for the cartoon 'Mr Magoo.' His portrayal of Mr Stark was his first serious motion picture role. The portrayal of 'Judy' was also former child star Natalie Wood's first adult role. She almost didn't get the part, because Ray was looking for 'authenticity.' But when a young man with a fresh knife scar on his face came to pick her up after the audition, Ray became more interested. It turned out that she was as mixed up in the world of gang fights and indifferent parents as any delinquent could be, and she was 'in.'

Dennis Hopper, playing a small part as Goon, was in much the same personal straights as Natalie, and most of the other 'gang members' were. Diminutive, soft spoken Sal Mineo, fresh from his first motion picture role – that of the juvenile phase of Tony Curtis' character in *Six Bridges to Cross* – seemed right for the part of the hypersensitive, neurotic Plato, who befriends Jim Stark. When James Dean discovered that Mineo was from the Bronx, his inveterate awe and deep love of New York City – his own adopted home – made for a strong rapport between the two actors, creating a situation that was perfect for their sympathetic roles.

Given Ray's directorial bias toward the ensemble approach, James

Dean had more of a burden toward wholly creating his character than would normally be the case even for a student of The Method. He mingled with gangs in Los Angeles, and found that most of the gangs had organized themselves according to movies they had seen, especially **The Wild One**. Dean said he felt a moral responsibility to give kids like those an alternative (as did Nicholas Ray also) – hence, the realistic complexity (although the parents are two-dimensional cliches) of **Rebel Without a Cause**, and its psychologically redemptive ending.

Years later, when he was called upon (and eventually declined) to narrate **The James Dean Story**, Marlon Brando said (with a hint of 'sour grapes'):

'[T]his glorifying of Dean is all wrong . . . I believe the documentary could be important . . . he wasn't a hero . . . just a lost boy trying to find himself . . . That ought to be done . . . maybe as a kind of expiation for some of my own sins. Like making **The Wild One**.'

Jimmy continued to date Ursula Andress, but the making of **Rebel Without a Cause** was taking up most of his time. Perhaps he threw himself into the project as a way of forgetting Pier Angeli, and of forgetting the news that Barbara Glenn had conveyed to him on his last sojourn – after wrapping up **East of Eden** – to New York.

Barbara was getting married. He demanded to meet the groom-to-be, and decided that Barbara had picked a good mate. Even so it didn't stop him from saying, 'You can't leave me, Barbara,' and throwing a tantrum when she reiterated that she could.

Likewise, he also alienated his old friend Dizzy Sheridan. When she teased him about having 'gone Hollywood,' he sulked for the whole night. James Dean, who was soon to prove himself a genius-level actor, did not quite know himself as an ordinary human being.

Still, instinctively, he sought out those sources of warmth that he had known: he returned to Fairmount on his way from New York back to Hollywood, spending a week in the company of his adopted 'mom and dad,' Ortense and Marcus Winslow.

Of course, his life had always been consumed with acting, and it was no surprise when he remarked to Hedda Hopper that he thought of the Winslow farm as 'a giant stage.' He also loved to play with cameras, taking photographer Dennis Stock with him, and between the two, they took hundreds of photographs – some of which would appear that same year as a James Dean documentary in *Life* magazine.

Among these photos were the mysterious ones of Jimmy laying in a casket, which was his way of tempting fate: the experience actually frightened him.

It was yet another example of his life as an outsider – he could taunt and tempt death, but due to his own stubborn individuality, was in the position

Above: James Dean, Method Actor, and self-taught non-Method actor Tab Hunter.
At far right: Jimmy hamming it up between takes. His expression here may well be reminiscent to some of his high school chums, who were privileged to see him in the Fairmount High production of *Goon With the Wind*, in which he played the Frankenstein monster.
Right: James Dean and Natalie Wood in a scene from *Rebel Without a Cause*. Wood's portrayal of Judy in this film was the former child star's first adult role.

of never really being able to pierce the veil, as he would accept no authority but his own on the subject. However, he chose to do his 'experiment' in familiar surroundings – the casket was one of several in stock at Hunt's General Store on Main Street in Fairmount.

Back on the West Coast, it was movie-making time again. The filming of **Rebel Without a Cause** began in March 1955. The 'gang members' of the cast were encouraged to live their lives as much together as they could, and Jimmy stayed away from all of them – to increase the sense of his alienation from them. The basic story line is as follows.

As the opening credits roll, we see Jim Stark lying dead drunk on a sidewalk, trying to cover a toy monkey he has found with a piece of trash, like a protective blanket. The scene is an improvisation that Dennis Hopper declared 'came from genius.' The police then arrest Jim and take him to the station, where Plato and Judy have already been brought: Plato has shot a puppy, and Judy has been wandering around, dressed like a prostitute.

On his first day at a new school, Jim attempts to make friends with 'the gang' during a class trip to the Griffith Planetarium. The gang decides to 'do' something about him, and the result is that Jimmy is goaded into a knife fight with Buzz, in the parking lot after the star show.

He and Buzz feint and jab at each other with their knives, and Jimmy wins the contest, only to receive another challenge: Buzz wants to 'play chicken'

Below: Natalie Wood, James Dean and Nicholas Ray confer during the filming of *Rebel Without a Cause.*
At right: Though never involved romantically, co-stars James Dean and Natalie Wood developed a close relationship during production.

821.

with him that night. In this contest, they are to drive stolen cars toward a precipice over the Pacific Ocean.

Jim goes home to get his dad's advice – a ritual with a foreordained end, for his father is terminally henpecked, and has always avoided his responsibilities as a man. In fact, both of Jim's parents are in the grip of post-war materialism: 'The war is over; there's plenty to eat; just don't rock the boat.' They've forgotten that they are parents.

His father is numbed to any condition but his own, and, as a result, his mother reacts as a 'predator,' in a subconscious attempt to get his father to respond with other than dead acquiescence, just once. The result of this terrible game is that Jim has never had a role model for manhood/adulthood, and is also the victim of his mother's vindictive anger, which colors his perception of girls and women, as well.

In the light of this latest crisis – the knife fight, bloody evidence of which stains Jim's shirt – his father once again tries to skirt the issue, and in this same scene, Jim sheds his brown jacket, and dons a bright red jacket – which serves as a warning (red for danger): Jim Stark is about to do something rash.

He storms out in frustration to meet Buzz for their contest. The winner of the game of 'chicken' is the one who leaps from his car last as the autos lunge over the cliff. Buzz gets his shirt caught on a door handle, and goes down with his car. Jim is stunned, and faces the moral dilemma: 'What should I do?' Likewise shocked, and seeking warmth, Judy, who was

At far left: A troubled Jim Stark after his eventful first day at school. Jim was forced into a knife fight by gang members after a class visit to the Griffith Planetarium.
Above: At the film's beginning, Jim's father, played by actor Jim Backus, is called to the police station to collect his son who has been arrested for public drunkenness.

Buzz' friend, rides home with Jim.

Later Jim has a confrontation with Plato. Jim chases him with Judy close behind. The police arrive, and Jim talks Plato into loaning him a pistol, from which he removes the bullets. He then coaxes Plato to come as far as the door, but Plato hesitates when he sees the police and the crowd that has gathered. 'They're not my friends!' he cries, and as he bolts away from Jim, the police shoot him dead.

Jim shouts, too late, 'But I've got the bullets!' He goes over to Plato and symbolically zips up his fallen friend's coat, 'to keep him warm.' Jim's dad says 'You did everything a man could.' And, having at last found out how to be a man by taking on the burden of responsibility, Jim Stark can now embark on the journey of adulthood.

The scene between Jim and Buzz just before the 'chicken run' was especially poignant for a generation seeking meaning. They're standing at the edge of the precipice, looking down at the ocean. Buzz says, 'I like you, you know?' to which Jim replies 'Buzz? What are we doing this for?' and Buzz replies: 'We got to do *something*. Don't we?'

The turning point of the film occurs when Jim confronts his father afterwards. Buzz is dead: something terrible and wrong has happened – and Jim wants to do something about it, but he doesn't quite know what to do.

Jimmy says 'Can I talk to you? . . . I've got to talk to somebody. Dad, you'd better give me an answer this time. A direct answer. You know that big, high bluff by Millertown . . . ?'

Below: **Between takes in the 'home' scene just after the chicken run. Jim has just come home, and cools his seething brain by rubbing the milk bottle across his forehead. He then drinks the entire contents of the bottle, like a child seeking the maternal solace of milk.**

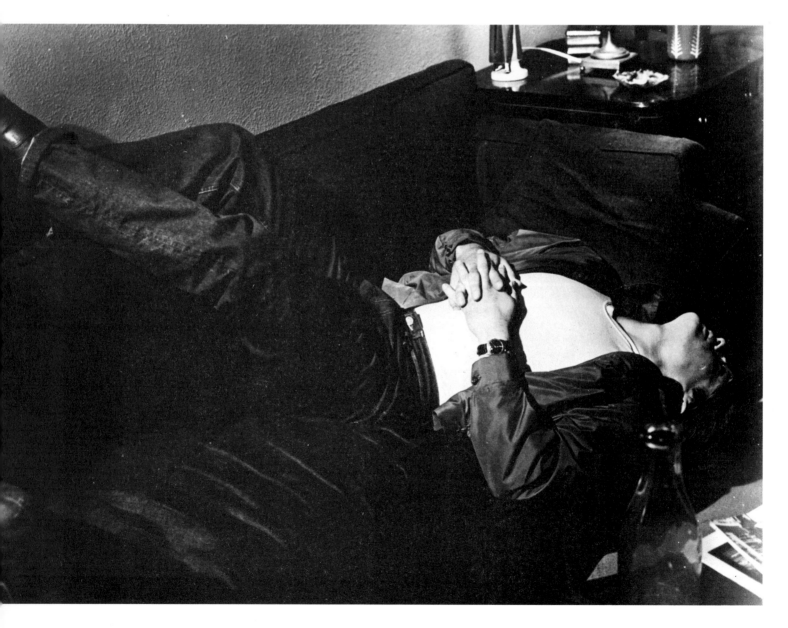

Above: Another ugly reality of Jim's life is that his mother has always avoided her motherly role. Her first words when he tells her about Buzz's death are 'Do you enjoy doing this to me?' Further, she does not want him to go to the police with his story: 'There were other people. Why should *you* be the only one involved?' He answers exasperatedly: 'But I *am* involved! We're *all* involved!'

At left: James Dean in Jim Stark's trademark tee-shirt between takes at the Griffith Planetarium.

Above: Plato, Jim and Judy in the mansion: Plato is beginning his 'tour guide' act. Soon, Jim and Judy say: 'Why don't we just rent it for the season?'
'[O]h, you tell him, darling . . .' 'Well, we're newlyweds.'

His dad says, 'Oh yes, there was a bad accident there. They showed the pictures on television, Jim.' 'I was in it. . . .' His mother begins a barrage of brutal irrelevancies that clearly reflect her self-concern: 'Do you enjoy doing this to me or what?' and both parents' answer to the overall question of *what to do about it* is 'Did anyone see you?'

That his father knew of Buzz's death only from the abstract medium of television – when his own son was directly involved – illustrates the utter vacuum that exists between them, and is an irony that is only compounded by the parents' recommendation that Jim act irresponsibly, by not going to the police about it.

That this is an inversion of normal familial roles needs not be dwelt upon. It does, however, set Jim up as the knight on a quest: even his 'closest advisors' have fallen under an evil spell, and it is up to him to heed the dictates of his conscience and to set the situation right.

This move toward doing the right thing eventually proves to be contagious – as Jim dashes into the planetarium in pursuit of Plato, his father prevents a nervous policeman from shooting him: once the 'spell' of moral lethargy is broken, his father, too, is freed.

The mother is also awakened into a better sensibility – when Jim

Below: Jim confronts the police after they have shot Plato down. Inside the planetarium, from which this penultimate scene emerges, Jim has surreptitously removed the bullets from Plato's gun. Of course, the police don't know that – until the fatal act has occurred. Jim Stark's words, as the gunshot reverberates in the night: 'But I've got the bullets!'

At left: Jim and Judy face his parents: 'Mom, dad, this is Judy. She's my friend.' Symbolically draped over his shoulder is his father's jacket – a sign that he has taken on the 'mantle' of adulthood.

introduces Judy as his 'friend,' both mother and father stand with the two youngsters in a harmonious, albeit shaken, family circle.

Rebel Without a Cause finished filming in May 1955. When it was released on 3 October 1955, James Dean was unanimously recognized as a major actor. Francois Truffaut said 'In James Dean, today's youth discovers itself. Less for the reasons usually advanced . . . than for others infinitely more simple and commonplace: modesty of feeling, moral purity. . . . eternal adolescent love of tests and trials . . . and regret at feeling oneself 'outside' of society. . . . '

James Dean had become the definitive portrayer of adolescent transition, and while *Rebel Without a Cause* won no formal awards, its immediate appeal to the youth of not only America, but the entire Western World, was immediate and lasting.

Most teenagers found *Rebel Without a Cause* to be a film that resonated with their own desire to find their way to adulthood.

While *Rebel Without a Cause* is James Dean's definitive film, he would perform a variation on similar themes in his next film – the huge, rambling epic *Giant*.

At left: James Dean and Director Nicholas Ray, on location near the Griffith Planetarium. *Rebel Without a Cause* is known worldwide as James Dean's definitive film. In it, he expressed the youthful questing for truth that is so important, and is too seldom served.

James Dean (*above*) enacted a voyage to adulthood with his character Jim Stark – and yet, even as he prepared to embark on his third and last cinematic triumph, the question lingers: had he found himself even then?

GIANT

Ain't nobody king in this country. Ain't nobody no matter what they might be thinkin'. – Jett Rink (James Dean).

Above and at right: On-location stills, between takes. The pain and suspicion in Jimmy's eyes are those of his character Jett Rink, in the Warner Brothers epic *Giant*. *Giant* was adapted from Edna Ferber's huge sprawling novel of the same name. Miss Ferber later said: 'James Dean was a genius. I don't think there's another actor in the world who could have portrayed Jett as well as he did.'

There was to be no relaxing for James Dean after *Rebel Without a Cause*. He had to go directly to work on his role as Jett Rink in *Giant*, a screen adaptation of Edna Ferber's epic novel. Jimmy had lobbied to get the part while he was still in preparation for *East of Eden*. He knew that George Stevens would be directing *Giant*, and he hungered for a chance to act under the then-legendary Stevens' direction.

Jimmy adopted the habit of dropping in on Stevens' assistant, Fred Guoil, with whom he talked cars. Guoil and Jimmy hit it off, but it was not until Stevens saw Jimmy's acting in *East of Eden* that he became a candidate for the role of Jett Rink.

Stevens later related, 'When *East of Eden* was finished, we went to see it, and the boy was just incredible. I'm not just talking about him as an actor, but it was his acting that made his personality so sensitive.' Stevens then offered the role to Jimmy, who said 'That'd be a good thing.'

Stevens was a vastly different kind of director than 'actor's directors' Ray and Kazan. Stevens saw actors as components in the whole of the production – they did as they were told, when they were told to do it.

There were problems between the two. Day after day, Jimmy sat waiting for his cues to do particular scenes. Sometimes he waited all day before the cue came. One day, the cue never came, for the scene was arbitrarily cut from that day's shooting schedule. The next day, Jimmy didn't show up on the set. Stevens was furious, and took him to Jack Warner's office, where the two really gave Jimmy a hard time, threatening to fire him from the film, and to throw him out of Hollywood.

Jimmy shot back: 'Are you finished? Well let me tell you something. I am not a machine . . . I prepared all night for that scene. I came in ready to work and you kept me sitting around all day . . . And you are not going to stop me from working.' It was something that might've been said by Jett Rink, the ranch hand who felt obliged to put 'the big shots' in their place.

Actor and director were from radically different schools: Stevens did not understand Method Acting, with its intensive emotional preparation: Jimmy was 'always in character' while filming a movie, yet he still had to undergo rigorous sessions of subjectively sinking deeper into character before doing a scene, in order to intensively 'imprint' that moment of the character's life.

Likewise, Dean didn't understand Stevens' 'old school' Hollywood-

style directing, which relied on actors taking up their characters without much emotional fuss until the scene began. It was a conflict that mirrored Jett Rink's tragic misunderstanding of the 'whys and the wherefores' of the wealthy Benedict family – whom he sought to emulate, even to supersede. He could only see the trappings of wealth and envy them; and while he himself might become immensely wealthy, he could never, ever *be* a Benedict.

The film was shot on location, in the environs of Marfa, Texas. The all-star cast included Rock Hudson (whose acting in **Magnificent Obsession** the year before had made him a 'hot property') as Texas rancher Bick Benedict; Elizabeth Taylor (already distinguished by over a dozen major motion picture roles) as Bick's wife, Leslie; Mercedes McCambridge (Academy Award winner for **All the King's Men**) as Bick's tough spinster sister, Luz; Dennis Hopper (fresh from his role in **Rebel Without a Cause**) as Bick's son, Jordy; Carroll Baker (who was then a rising star on stage and television) as Bick's daughter Luz II; Sal Mineo (fresh from his extraordinary performance as Plato in **Rebel Without a Cause**) as the Mex-Tex war hero, Angel; and Elsa Cardenas (already gaining renown as a character actress) as Jordy's wife, Juana. Veteran actor Chill Wills played Bick Benedict's lawyer.

The story opens with Bick Benedict's trip to Virginia, where he plans to

At left: A publicity still for *Giant*, featuring Rock Hudson and Elizabeth Taylor, in costume as Bick and Leslie Benedict. Liz Taylor came to like James Dean as a friend. Rock Hudson, on the other hand, declared him 'surly and angry,' further adding that Dean had 'no manners.' One suspects sour grapes, touched by a tinge of truth.
Above: Elizabeth Taylor and James Dean in a publicity still for *Giant*. She seems to keen for doomed Jett, who is here seen 'crucified' on his own ambitions.

Above: **A between-takes still of Jett, with his defender and champion at the Reata Ranch – Bick Benedict's tough spinster sister Luz. Luz Benedict was capably portrayed by Mercedes McCambridge.**
At right: **Jett brings news of an oil gusher at Little Reata: 'I'm rich, Bick. . . . I'm going to be richer than all you sons of Benedicts!'**

buy a Thoroughbred from a famous breeder. He buys the horse, and in the course of sociable negotiations, falls in love with Leslie, the horse breeder's daughter. They marry – and horse, bride and groom return to Bick's Reata Ranch in Texas.

The Reata Ranch is essentially a gigantic dusty plain with a huge weather beaten Victorian mansion in the middle of it. Bick's tough sister, Luz, takes an immediate dislike to the genteel Leslie, even assigning Bick and his bride separate rooms when they first arrive. It's obvious that Luz runs the ranch.

Leslie takes some time to get used to Texas, her first shock being the incredible expanse of the Texas flatlands, her second being her hostess, and her third being the shy yet surly hired hand Jett Rink. While Bick is continually trying to fire Jett, Luz stubbornly keeps him on the staff.

One day, Luz dies in an accident while riding Bick's new horse. Almost ironically, her motherly attitude toward the dispossessed Jett is amplified by her last will and testament. She leaves Jett 10 acres of scrub land called 'Buffalo Wallow,' not far from the Reata ranch house. Despite Bick's offer of $1200 for this piece of apparently worthless land, Jett turns Bick down, out of sentimental concern for 'old Madame,' as he called Luz.

He calls the place 'Little Reata.'

As Bick is busy putting his sister's affairs in order, Leslie betakes herself to a nearby Mexican village, where the sickness and poverty of the people breaks her heart. She embarks on a covert career of tending to the poor and ill in the village. One of her charges, a little boy named Angel, is eventually to grow up and become a war hero.

On her way back to Reata after one of her sojourns in the village, she stops at Little Reata to say hello to Jett, and a peaceful visit ensues. As she is getting back into her car, she slips a little in the mud, and oil starts oozing from the divot she makes with her foot. Jett hires a drilling rig and soon makes a big oil strike.

Now a millionaire, he forms the Jettexas Company, builds a motel and airport complex, and generally becomes the most important man in the region. Meanwhile, the Benedicts produce three children: Jordy, Judy and Luz II. We pick up the tale again after several decades have passed.

The idealistic Jordy, to Bick's disappointment, does not want to follow in his father's footsteps. He wants to be a doctor, and, in harmony with his mother's non-racist attitude, wants to marry Juana, a Tex-Mex girl. His parents have no objections to this, especially since Angel's body has just been sent home from Korea, and the Tex-Mex boy is buried as a bona fide American war hero.

At right: Jett spots Leslie driving by, and fires off a shot to get her attention, by way of inviting her to tea. *Above:* Once inside, Leslie looks over the grammar and self-improvement books that Jett is reading. Jett looks on, warily searching for signs of approval.

Rock Hudson was continually upstaged by James Dean during the filming of *Giant*, and he hated that even more than he disliked James Dean himself. Some purposeful irritation may well have been supplied by Jimmy, as he would have thought such resentment would help to inform their antagonistic characterizations.

At right: Jimmy upstages Rock in an off-camera activity applying 'the old rope trick' to Elizabeth Taylor, who appreciated Jimmy for the brilliant, eccentric person he was. Rock is clearly not enjoying himself here, and perhaps commenting on her playfully entwined state, gives Ms Taylor a questioning look of disapproval. James Dean, on the other hand, was absorbed in improving his grasp on Jett Rink's character: he learned roping, horseback riding, hunting and other cowboy skills, and perfected a West Texas drawl through careful observation of the inhabitants of the Marfa locale, and sessions with dialogue coach Bob Hinckle.

To reflect his status Jett makes his 'Reata' a thing gilded with all the glossy trappings that commercial civilization has to offer – a combination motel and airport!

He might have been happier with a ranch, or in helping other struggling ranch hands get a foothold. Jett is not all bad – just confused. In the scene at 'Little Reata,' he displayed a tenderness and an integrity that he later abandoned, to his detriment, when he fell further into the trap described above. It's very telling that the word 'reata' means 'lariat' – an item that can be of great use to a cowboy, or can be used as a noose from which to hang him.

The name 'Jett Rink' can likewise be interpreted as 'fast surface' – a slippery skating surface, treacherous, but also allowing one to make great progress – or a 'black circle' – the traditional symbol of bad luck.

Going back to Ms Ferber's comment on success poisoning, did James Dean have 'an insatiable need for power and recognition'? He was certainly busy – three pictures in two years, and he had signed a contract with Warner Brothers for nine more pictures in the following six years.

His career ambitions also were tending toward branching out. He'd been talking with Nicholas Ray about forming their own production company, (their first corporate collaboration was to have been **Dr Jekyll and Mr Hyde**), and in an interview with Hedda Hopper, he stated:

'Acting is wonderful . . . but my talents lie in directing and, beyond that, my great fear is writing . . . I can't apply the seat of my pants right now. I'm too youthful and silly. I must have some age. I'm in great awe of writing . . . but some day. . . . '

As far as wanting recognition, he both flirted with it and denied it (thus generating more publicity): 'Who needs it? What counts to the artist is performance, not publicity.'

At any rate, his relations with George Stevens improved when Hedda Hopper informed him that Stevens was in a partnership with Edna Ferber and financier Henry Ginsberg, and that Jimmy's relations with Stevens therefore involved more than his own immediate career: if the production flopped, Ginsberg would take a terrible loss. Still, there was tension, even though Stevens later said '[H]e really knew that character. And that's the best tribute that I can pay to his talent as an actor.'

Illustrative of Jimmy's acumen is the famous scene in the movie when Bick Benedict comes over and leans on the car, by way of telling Jett to clear out.

Jett pulls his hat over his eyes. This move is Jimmy's invention, and is thus explained by Lee Strasberg: 'You see every actor doing it now . . . pulling his hat down . . . it's become a style. But there was nothing loose about it . . . when Jim did it. Inside he was saying 'Gee, that blankety-blank,' but he couldn't quite say it. So he pulled down that hat. . . . '

Though Jimmy shared a house with Rock Hudson and Chill Wills for the three months of on-location shooting, relations between the two leading actors were continually frosty even in their off hours. Hudson later said:

'Dean was hard to be around . . . never smiled . . . had no manners. And he was rough to do a scene with . . . in the giving and taking . . . he was just a taker.' This is in countervention to comments made by other actors who had worked with Jim, who nearly unanimously agreed that he was intense, and often intensely helpful to their own efforts.

A Method Actor always, it is probable that Jimmy was purposely upping the animosity quotient between himself and Hudson, so that 'Bick' and 'Jett' would fairly crackle with that tension. For the entire time of production, he was never out of character. As soon as the cast arrived on location in Marfa, he donned his 'Jett Rink' outfit: cowboy boots, Levis, vest, denim shirt and Stetson. With help from dialogue coach Bob Hinckle, he took on a regional drawl and developed such cowboy skills as range riding, playing guitar and twirling a lariat.

Despite their differences, he became quite close with director Stevens, and co-star Elizabeth Taylor was extremely fond of him.

At right: Director George Stevens and James Dean at a pre-production meeting, with an oil well model in evidence to echo the central catalyst of *Giant.*

Above: The hardened look of determination on Jett Rink's face has a prophetic, tragic quality – as if Jett already discerns his failure, born out of that same determination.

Giant was released on 11 October 1956. Warner Brothers actually feared the audience response to the film, as James Dean had, by then, a huge and fanatical following.

EPILOGUE

Above: James Dean behind the wheel of his first
car, a used MG roadster that he bought in May
1954. The MG was also his first sports car, and
with it, Jimmy developed an interest in sports car
racing. This meshed emotionally with his interest
in the bull ring, and the mortal danger to be
confronted there.
Hence, we have a Warner Brothers publicity
portrait (*at right*) of James Dean as a death-
defying toreador.

When *Giant* opened after more than a year of cutting and edit-
ing, James Dean the person would be just a memory and an
ache in the heart of his many friends and acquaintances.
James Dean the *symbol of questing adolescence*, however, would be
just beginning an unprecedented reign as the center of youthful emula-
tion around the world.

His death was born of his own desire to push on, to test the limits. He
loved sports car racing. In May 1954, he'd bought an MG roadster, and
getting the feel of it, desired to get a bit more involved with motor sports.
He sold the MG and bought a white Porsche Speedster, which he
entered in California Sports Car Club races, running in the 'D' Production class. Sports columnist Wilson Springer's first reaction to Jimmy's
racing was '[T]his guy really knows how to handle his car.'

In fact, Jimmy won a number of races. Race car mechanic Ken Miles
said, 'Jimmy wanted speed,' but added that he would never have been
a great driver, because his concentration was predominately on speed,
and less on knowing how to maneuver his car.

Still, his keenness was such that when he was introduced to famous
motorcycle racer Ed Kretz, Jimmy said 'Jeez, you mean "Iron Man" Ed
Kretz? . . . It's certainly a thrill to meet you, Ed. I saw you in 1946 at
Hamilton, Indiana . . . you really blew those guys off the track . . .' and
gushed on like any ardent fan.

Jimmy's last race was in May 1955, when, due to engine failure, he
was forced to pull out of competition.

During the filming of **Giant**, he did a safety film with Gig Young for the
National Highway Committee. The punch line of the film was 'And remember, drive safely, for the life you save may be -' and here Jimmy
altered the speech from 'your own' to '*mine.*'

Not long after, Jimmy bought a Porsche Spyder, capable of 150 mph,
solely for racing.

On 30 September 1955, Jimmy and mechanic Rudolph Wutherich
(from whom he had bought the car) got in the Spyder and headed north
from Los Angeles, toward Salinas, where Jimmy would drive the Spyder
in its first race. At 3:30 pm that same day, California Highway Patrolman
Oscar Hunter pulled Jimmy over for doing 65 in a 45 mph zone.

Twilight settled over the highway at 5:30 pm, and at 5:45 pm, James
Dean was mortally injured when his speeding silver Porsche slammed
into the side of a Ford sedan driven by Donald Turnupseed, who had
been making a left-hand turn onto Route 466.

The accident occurred at the intersection of routes 466 and 41, near Cholame, California.

Turnupseed had abrasions and a concussion, and suffered from shock. Jimmy's companion, Wutherich, was injured in being thrown free from the Porsche. James Dean was pinned in the wreckage of his car. His neck and numerous other bones in his crumpled body were broken. Just 24 years old, he died shortly after the accident.

His friends were devastated. Elizabeth Taylor literally fell into a swoon and was weeks recovering. George Stevens wept as if his own son had died. Ortense and Marcus Winslow were returning to Fairmount, Indiana, after visiting Jimmy in Los Angeles. They were thunderstruck when they heard of Jimmy's death.

Winton Dean, himself a tragic figure ever since the loss of Jim's mother, traveled with Jimmy's body to Fairmount, where the entire town had draped itself in mourning for its well-remembered and most famous son. The funeral took place on 8 October 1955, and was attended by 3000 people. The entire population of Fairmount was only 2000.

Rebel Without a Cause opened on 3 October 1955, and the newspaper reviews of the film were full of such commentary as: 'He stands out as a re-markable talent . . . he was cut down by the same passions he exposes so tellingly in this strange and forceful picture.' 'In this movie, he wins an auto race with death. Only four weeks ago . . . he lost one.'

Then, in December 1955, Jimmy began receiving posthumous acco-

At left: A rather dressed-up James Dean sits casually, but with intent stare, atop the driver's door of his Porsche Speedster.

Below: James Dean and a crowd of admirers examine some of his racing trophies in a Warner Brothers promotional still taken during the advertising blitz for *Rebel Without a Cause*. Jimmy was quite pleased to be winning regularly, though it made George Stevens so nervous that he got him to give up racing for the duration of *Giant*'s production.

lades for his work in **East of Eden**. He was awarded the Council of Motion Picture Organizations' First Audience Award for Best Perforance of the Year; and in February 1956, *Photoplay* magazine named him Best Actor of 1955. He was also nominated for an Academy Award as 'Best Actor.'

Preparing for the release of **Giant** on 11 October 1956, Warner Brothers was almost afraid to publicize the film. Since Jimmy's death, they received letters from around the world expressing a nearly hysterical resentment that he had died just when his fans were getting to know him.

His next roles for Warner Brothers were to have been Billy the Kid in **Left-Handed Gun**, and Rocky Graziano in **Somebody Up There Likes Me**.

In 1956, George Stevens won a 'Best Director' Academy Award for his work on **Giant**, and for *his* work in the same motion picture, a posthumous nomination as Best Actor was made for James Dean.

When the end credits of **Giant** were indeed rolling in a neighborhood movie theater, somewhere on the planet Earth, sometime in the last four decades, one anonymous teenager spoke for many when she cried: 'Come back, Jimmy Dean!'

At left: Jimmy and the Speedster. He was his own pit crew most of the time, and his entourage usually consisted of two Warner Brothers publicists, seeking to make the most of the young star's every waking moment.

Above: James Dean in his Porsche Spyder. He would die in this car on 30 September 1955, en route to a race in Salinas. Ironically, four days after – on 3 October 1955 – *Rebel Without a Cause* opened, and a legend that was already forming erupted into a life of its own.

JAMES DEAN
1931Feb8 – 1955Sep30pm5:59 ∞

Above: A monument, near the accident site where James Dean lost his life. He was just 24 years old when he and Rolf Wutherich slammed into Donald Turnupseed's Ford sedan, at the intersection of California routes 41 and 466.
Fans throughout the world reacted vehemently to the loss of a star they were only beginning to know. He was buried in Fairmount, Indiana, on 8 October 1955. *At right:* James Dean – his end came too swiftly, and the echoes remain.

INDEX